The White House belongs to you a[nd]
citizens. It is a government building
over it. Every four years, voters deci[de]
live there.

How many
windows do
you count?

I'M ABBY. MEMBERS OF
OUR FAMILY WERE LIVING
ON THE GROUNDS EVEN
BEFORE IT WAS BUILT.

WELCOME!

With special appreciation to
Rex Scouten
Former Curator of the White House

ISBN: 0-8362-2153-2

Author: Betty Debnam
Editor: Jake Morrissey
Designer: Betty Debnam
Production: Angela Farley
Illustration: Wendy Jamieson
Word Puzzles: Anne Chamberlain
Editorial Assistance: Alan McDermott, Lucy Lien

White House Historical Association
Hugh S. Sidey
Chairman

Staff
President: Neil W. Horstman
Coordinating Editor: Maria Downs
Illustrations Research: Patricia McCloskey
Production coordinator: Donald J. Crump

The White House Historical Association is a nonprofit organization chartered on November 3, 1961, to enhance understanding, appreciation, and enjoyment of the White House.

04 05 06 07 MLT 11 10 9 8

A KID'S GUIDE TO THE WHITE HOUSE

Betty Debnam

Produced in cooperation with

THE WHITE HOUSE

HISTORICAL ASSOCIATION

Andrews McMeel
Publishing

Kansas City

Welcome
to the
White House

George Washington's White House

This picture shows George Washington inspecting the building of the White House.

George Washington played an important part in our country's early history and in the building of the White House. "The father of our country" could also be called "the father of the White House."

Washington knew that the leader of our new country and those who would follow would need a very special place to live and work.

Washington was the only president who never lived in the White House. He was out of office before it was finished.

Selecting the Site

The White House, where our president lives, is in Washington, D.C., the capital city of the United States. George Washington chose the site in 1791.

George Washington and other signers of the Constitution in 1787.

The city of Washington was to be a special area carved out of two states, Maryland and Virginia. The area was to be called the District of Columbia.

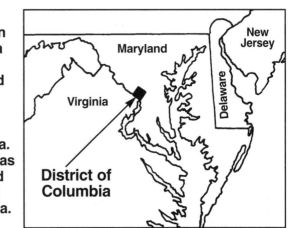

Today we use the initials "D.C."

George Washington, the great hero of the American Revolution, was president of the convention that wrote our Constitution, or plan of government.

He was also our first president. One of the first things the new government did was to make plans for a capital city. It was to be named for Washington. The plans included a home for the president while he was in office.

This is the city map that L'Enfant drew up for Washington in 1800.

Can you find the White House?

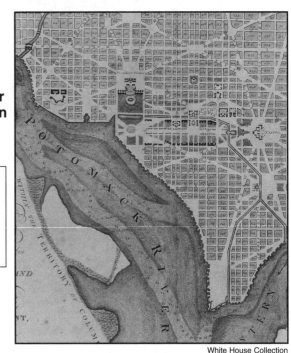

White House Collection

Pierre Charles L'Enfant

George Washington chose Pierre Charles L'Enfant, who was from France, to design the city. He fought in the Revolutionary War with Washington. Two Americans, Andrew Elliott and Benjamin Banneker, surveyed and measured the streets.

A star marks Washington, D.C.

Today the White House is in a big park called the President's Park. Government buildings, hotels and monuments are in the neighborhood. The White House has additions, or wings, that have been added to each side.

photo by Erik Kvalsvik, courtesy White House Historical Association

WASHINGTON IS A CITY OF WIDE STREETS AND PARKS WITH LOTS OF TREES!

The city of Washington is one of the few capitals in the world that was planned before it was built. It is also the only town or city in the United States that is not a part of a state.

Building the White House

George Washington was very interested in planning and building the home for the president. He wanted to build a house that would "last beyond the present day." And it has.

Washington chose the winner of a contest held to decide who would design it. He selected James Hoban as the architect.

This painting shows the site near the Potomac River that Washington selected for the President's House.

Washington visited the building site. It was not far from his Virginia home Mount Vernon.

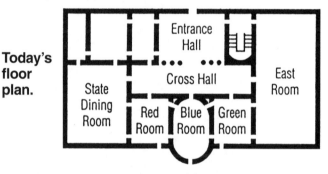

Today's floor plan.

Entrance Hall
Cross Hall
State Dining Room
Red Room
Blue Room
Green Room
East Room

This is the original plan of the main floor. Notice how it is very much like the plan of today. Notice the oval room. (The big black spot is a hole in the paper.)

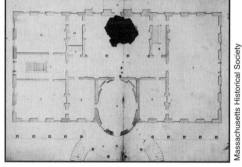

Washington liked oval-shaped rooms. As guests stood in a circle, he would walk around and speak to each one.

Hoban won a medal for his design of the "President's House." Washington liked the rectangle shape because it was one that could be added to easily.

James Hoban was born in Ireland.

If Washington were to visit the White House today, he probably would recognize the building.

Scout It Out!

Can you find:

- ruler
- hammer
- number 3
- dragon
- book
- carrot
- bell
- kite
- ladder
- toothbrush
- flashlight
- exclamation mark
- hairbrush
- fish
- letter D

The same outside walls of the President's House that Washington watched being built still stand today. Since then, in the 200 years that followed, the United States and the number of its citizens have grown greatly.

**1789
4 million Americans**

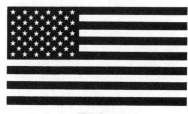

**Today
260 million Americans**

Finishing the White House

Building the home for the president took eight years, from 1792 to 1800. The outside walls are made of stone taken from a quarry in nearby Virginia. The inside walls were lined with bricks. The bricks were made on the grounds, using soil from the site.

courtesy National Park Service Historic American Buildings Survey

The stonemasons of more than 200 years ago carved many beautiful designs, such as this one over the door that faces Pennsylvania Avenue.

The workers who placed the stones were paid by how many they laid, so they carved their own marks in them. We can still see some of the marks today.

courtesy White House Historical Association

photo by Betty Debnam

A visitor watches as a stonemason of today carves a new stone for the White House. It takes a lot of work to keep a building more than 200 years old in good shape.

To do: If you were a stone-mason at the White House, what might your special mark be? Draw it here.

The White House was first painted in 1798, two years before it was finished. The sandstone it is made of cracks. Painting it keeps it from cracking even more.

A drawing of how the White House looked in 1807, seven years after it was finished.

To celebrate the start of some important buildings, a special ceremony is held. It is called "the laying of the cornerstone."

The cornerstone for the President's House was laid on Oct. 13, 1792. A special brass plate with the date on it was sealed between two of the foundation stones.

To celebrate the 200th birthday of the White House in 1992, experts tried to find the brass plate, but its whereabouts remain a mystery.

Abby's Word Search

The building words that Abby is holding are hidden in the sentences below. We have found the first one for you. See if you can find the rest.

1. <u>Who used</u> the oven?
2. Bob, Rick and I went to the movie.
3. We were just on East Street.
4. Those are two odd shoes.
5. The car very slowly drove away.
6. We saw Al leave the house.
7. Is Papa in trouble?
8. There's the fellow in green pants.

BRICK
STONE
WALL
PAINT
CARVE
HOUSE
WOOD
WING

Answers: 1. house, 2. brick, 3. stone, 4. wood, 5. carve, 6. wall, 7. paint, 8. wing.

After 200 years, parts of the White House had to be covered in 1992 while workers repaired the stonework and removed 42 layers of paint.

Settling In

President John Adams greets his wife as she arrives at the unfinished White House.

This artist's impression of the White House shows the colonnades very well. However, the grounds weren't very pretty. Much of the land toward the river was swampy.

John Adams

Abigail Adams

John Adams, the second president, was the first to live in the White House.

When John and Abigail Adams moved into the White House in November of 1800, it still wasn't finished. Many of the rooms were cold and damp. "Shiver, shiver," Mrs. Adams complained.

The Adamses did not live there long. His term ended four months after he moved in.

Thomas Jefferson was the next president to move in. After Jefferson came James Madison. Slowly the White House began to feel like a home.

Thomas Jefferson

Thomas Jefferson finished adding these colonnades, or low wings, in 1808. They were used for stables, servants' quarters, work and storage areas.

When Thomas Jefferson moved into the White House, he did not bring along his family. His wife had died and his daughters were grown.

Like many presidents, Thomas Jefferson enjoyed having his grandchildren visit him. James Madison Randolph, his grandson, was the first child born in the White House. He was born when his mother, Martha, was visiting.

Jefferson liked entertaining and fine living. His daughter Martha often served as his hostess.

Martha Jefferson Randolph

1970 Louis S. Glanzman

Lewis and Clark also sent back a stuffed magpie, a type of bird, and a prairie dog. Jefferson sent these to a museum.

Jefferson was interested in many subjects, including animals. He brought some unusual ones to the White House.

When the explorers Lewis and Clark went west, they sent back examples of the strange, new animals that people in Washington had never seen. Another explorer, Zebulon Pike, sent two grizzly bear cubs. Jefferson put them on display in specially built cages placed on the South Lawn.

Jefferson had a pet mockingbird named Dick. Jefferson trained him to sing along while he played the violin. Dick would also hop along, step by step, when Jefferson went upstairs.

13

The Fire and Rebuilding

In 1814, when James Madison was president, a terrible thing happened. The White House was burned by the British. We were at war because the British were interfering with our shipping. The Americans also felt that the British were urging the Indians to attack western settlers.

Only a heavy rain saved the White House from being burned to the ground in the fire on Aug. 24, 1814.

courtesy Mac G. Morris Collection

photo courtesy Smithsonian Institution

White House Collection

Dolley Madison, the president's wife, fled the White House just before the British arrived. She took with her the portrait of George Washington (right). It was painted by Gilbert Stuart, a famous American painter.

This portrait of George Washington is the oldest object belonging to the White House. It hangs in the East Room.

White House Collection

President James Madison was known as "the great little Madison." He is called "the Father of our Constitution." At only 100 pounds and 5 feet 4 inches tall, he was our smallest president.

14

Look in the background of this painting to see the burned-out shell of the White House. The building in the front is St. John's Church. It still stands today across the park from the White House.

After the fire, the White House was just a burned-out shell. It took three years to rebuild it to the way it was. President James Monroe moved in in 1817.

Several years later, in 1824, the South Portico, or porch, was added. This view faces the "big back yard."

The North Portico was added in 1829. This side of the White House faces Pennsylvania Avenue. It is considered the White House's "front porch."

15

Adding the Wings

For many years, the president's offices and the family living areas were on the same floor. The president's staff, Cabinet members and people seeking jobs and favors came upstairs. The president's family had very little privacy.

THE PRESIDENT LIVED AND WORKED UPSTAIRS!

Years ago, people wanting to see the president waited their turn inside the White House.

April 7, 1877, Frank Leslie's Illustrated Newspaper

Something had to be done about the crowded conditions. Upstairs, the White House was just too small for both the president's office and the president's family. When President Theodore Roosevelt moved in with his six children, he asked for more office space. An addition, called the West Wing, was built. The Oval Office was added later.

A U.S. Marine is one of the guards on duty outside the West Wing.

© Bill Fitz-Patrick

The West Wing in 1902, after it was completed. Thousands of people work for the president, but only a few work in the West Wing.

courtesy Library of Congress

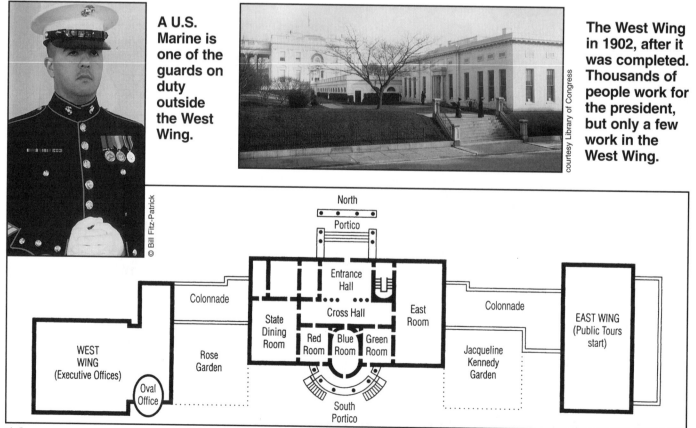

North
Portico

Entrance Hall

Cross Hall

Colonnade

State Dining Room

Red Room

Blue Room

Green Room

East Room

Colonnade

EAST WING (Public Tours start)

WEST WING (Executive Offices)

Rose Garden

Oval Office

Jacqueline Kennedy Garden

South Portico

In 1902, the East Wing was added as a visitors entrance. In the 1800s, most of the White House guests came in and left through the North Portico, or front door.

Today thousands of visitors enter through the East Wing every day.

Before the East Wing entrance was added, some events were so packed that guests left through a window over a wooden bridge set up outside the East Room.

Today's visitors enter a paneled lobby in the East Wing.

How the White House grew

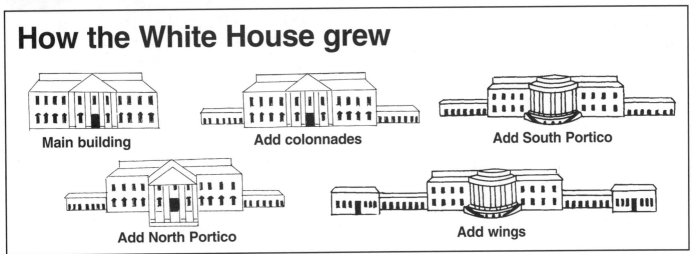

Main building

Add colonnades

Add South Portico

Add North Portico

Add wings

Redoing the Inside

While people took good care of the White House, it still began to show signs of wear and needed repair. In 1948, something happened to call attention to the shape that it was in. The leg of a piano that belonged to Margaret Truman, the president's daughter, went right through the floor. Someone said that the White House had been "standing purely out of habit." Something had to be done.

Later that year, experts discovered that the White House wasn't safe. It was totally gutted and renovated. The outside walls remained, but everything inside was replaced. Two new basements were added. A new concrete and steel frame was put in place. The number of rooms was increased from about 65 to 132.

Only the outside walls remained when the White House was gutted.

The Trumans moved back in March of 1952. President Truman was very pleased. He later gave a tour of the new house on TV.

President Harry S. Truman was a very hard worker. He is famous for the sign on his desk that read "THE BUCK STOPS HERE." That means that the president is responsible for what happens while he is in office.

18

Adding a balcony

President Truman also wanted a place where he could sit outside. In 1948, before the White House was gutted, he added a balcony to the South Portico.

Some people didn't like the idea of a balcony, but President Truman insisted. Since then, other White House families have enjoyed it very much.

I LIKE THIS IDEA.

President Dwight D. "Ike" Eisenhower was the next president after Truman. In this photo, he waves to his wife, Mamie, as she stands on the "Truman Balcony."

United Press International

Go dot to dot and color.

First Families and Their Kids

The president and his family live on the second floor of the White House. Over the years, third-floor bedrooms and a large family room, called a "solarium," have been added. This is the most informal room in the White House. It has a beautiful view overlooking the South Lawn.

Franklin D. Roosevelt and Eleanor Roosevelt (far left) pose with their 13 grandchildren. This photo was taken before ceremonies marking the fourth time he was sworn in as president.

Out of respect, we call the family who lives in the White House our "first family." We call the president's wife the "first lady." We often call the children the "first kids." We wonder what their private life can be like in such a public place.

Most presidents have children or grandchildren who live in the White House or who often visit.

President Franklin Roosevelt lived in the White House longer than any other president. He served for three full terms, or 12 years. He died two months after being sworn in for his fourth term.

Baby McGee holds the reins for His Whiskers, a goat presented to him by his grandfather, President Benjamin Harrison.

Mrs. Mamie Eisenhower watches a movie with her grandchildren in the White House theater.

Kids who grow up in the White House have many advantages. They don't have to do housework. They meet movie stars. People are thrilled to see them.

You might wish to be a White House kid, because all of this looks like such fun with so many wonderful things to do.

However, being famous does have its problems. First kids get lots of attention. Everybody is watching. There is little privacy. A Secret Service agent is with you outside the White House. What you do makes the news.

But through it all, being a White House kid is a great opportunity and privilege. In the next few pages, you'll meet some of the younger children of first families.

Marshall Bush (the girl closest to Ranger, the dog), granddaughter of President George Bush, celebrates her fifth birthday on the South Lawn.

President John Tyler had more children (15) than any other president. Of the eight children by his first wife, only four lived in the White House. His seven children by his second wife were born after he left office.

The Lincolns

When the Lincolns moved into the White House in 1861, they had three children: Tad, age 7; Willie, age 10; and Robert, age 17.

Willie and Tad were the first children of a president to live in the White House in a long time. The boys often played pranks that helped cheer up the president. They also had many pets, including ponies, dogs and goats.

Abraham Lincoln and his wife, Mary, were loving parents. "Let the children have a good time," they said, and the younger children usually did.

An engraving of the Lincoln family: Tad, Mary, Robert, Willie and the president.

White House Collection

Tad in a child-size colonel's Army uniform.

courtesy National Archives

Tad in a photo with his father, taken in 1864.

courtesy Louis A. Warren Lincoln Library and Museum, Fort Wayne, Indiana

A SAD, SAD TIME.

President Lincoln was especially close to his son Willie, who died just before his 12th birthday. Mrs. Lincoln never recovered from the loss.

Lincoln spent most of his time in the White House overseeing the Union forces during the Civil War. One of the things he did was to sign the Emancipation Proclamation. This document freed all of the slaves in the states that were rebelling against the Union forces.

This painting shows the first reading of the Emancipation Proclamation. The event took place on July 22, 1862, in the White House in what is now the Lincoln Bedroom.

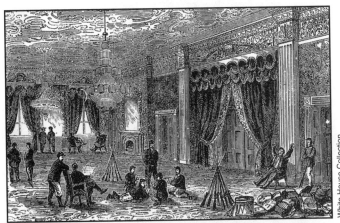

In the early days of the Civil War, Union troops camped out in the White House East Room. The Lincoln family lived on the floor above.

When Lincoln was assassinated, his casket was put on display in the East Room. Hundreds of people came to pay their respects.

Abraham Lincoln was the first president to be assassinated. He died on April 15, 1865, a little over a month after he had begun his second term.

The Theodore Roosevelts

"I don't think that any family has ever enjoyed the White House more than we have," Theodore Roosevelt wrote. The Roosevelts moved into the White House in 1901.

President Roosevelt, his wife and six children.

Roosevelt's oldest daughter, Alice, was married in the White House. The wedding was a big social event.

President Roosevelt had an older daughter, Alice, and five younger children, ranging in age from 3 to 13 when they moved in, in 1901. The children played everywhere throughout the house and had many pets.

When the president, whom they called "T.R.," was not too busy, he liked playing with them, too.

Theodore Roosevelt Jr. had a macaw named Eli Yale. Roosevelt pets included a pony, raccoons, snakes, cats, badgers and dogs.

Theodore Roosevelt made the White House the official name in 1901. Before that time its official name was the President's House and then the Executive Mansion.

24

Archie Roosevelt salutes as his brother Quentin stands at ease during a roll call of the White House police.

Teddy Roosevelt has a toy named for him. Once while he was hunting, he refused to shoot a bear. A newspaper cartoonist drew a picture showing this incident. The bear became famous. A toy maker started making bears, and called them "Teddy."

Quentin Roosevelt on his pony, Algonquin.

The "pet" pet story of the White House is about Quentin and his pony, Algonquin. One day, Quentin put Algonquin in the White House elevator and took him up to see his sick brother Archie.

The Kennedys

Caroline and John Kennedy Jr. were the first young children of a president to live in the White House in more than 50 years. They moved into the White House in January 1961 with their parents, John and Jacqueline Kennedy.

People were very interested in the Kennedy children and their glamorous parents.

Caroline and her younger brother "John John" in her second-floor bedroom at the White House.

The public carefully watched everything that first lady Jacqueline Kennedy did. She set many fashion trends.

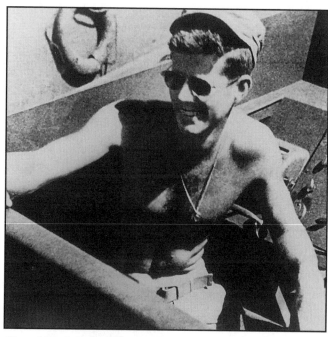

President John Kennedy was a World War II hero who had served in the U.S. Senate before being elected president.

At the age of 43, John Kennedy was the youngest president ever elected. But the youngest person ever to be president was Theodore Roosevelt, who took office when McKinley was assassinated. Roosevelt was 42.

Caroline Kennedy had a pet pony named Macaroni. She sometimes rode Macaroni on the South Lawn of the White House. The Kennedy children also had a pet canary and a dog that was a gift from the Soviet Union.

This is a famous photo of "John John" playing under his father's desk in the Oval Office. This spot was his favorite hiding place.

It was another sad day for the country when President Kennedy's casket was carried from the White House. He was assassinated on Nov. 22, 1963, just two years and 10 months after being sworn into office.

Mrs. Kennedy wanted to keep her children away from a lot of public attention. She started a kindergarten at the White House for Caroline.

27

A Talk with Susan Ford

Gerald Ford Presidential Library

Susan with Shan, her Siamese cat.

Susan Ford was a senior in a high school nearby in Maryland when her family moved into the White House in 1974. She did not have to change schools. Her father, Gerald Ford, had been a U.S. congressman for many years.

What's it like to live there?

"It's like a fairy tale," Susan said. "The people you meet — the kings, queens and movie stars — and the experiences.

"The first time my friends visited me, they were probably impressed, but they got used to it."

Service

"The service is absolutely delightful. You can be waited on hand and foot if you want that. You can be left alone if you want that.

"It's always fresh towels and fresh sheets and the food is delivered to your room.

"If Mother and Dad were at an event, I'd have the food brought upstairs to my room.

"I don't think my mother wanted me to become a little princess or a prima donna," Susan said. "She said that 'Susan will still get up in the morning and make her bed every day,' and so I did."

Privacy

"If you're in your room on the third floor, you have as much privacy as any kid who goes in her room and closes the door. I was not conscious of tourists going through downstairs. I didn't even think about it."

White House Collection

Gerald Ford is the only person to serve as both vice president and president of the United States without being elected to either office. He was appointed to the office of vice president by Richard Nixon. He took over as president when Nixon resigned.

Susan is standing next to the guest in a white jacket (upper right of photo). She is wearing flowers.

About the prom

"It was very special to have my senior prom at the White House," she said. "The government didn't pay for it. All the girls also helped do flower arrangements. Of course we had a complete turnout. Everybody showed up."

Room decorating

"You can decorate your room any way you want to at your parents' expense. I could stick up things on the walls. They have a warehouse full of furniture you can choose from."

Favorite room

"I think the room I used most was the solarium. That was to me more normal. It did not have antiques. It was bright yellow ... a more typical family room. Plus it had an absolutely gorgeous view of Washington."

The beautiful view from Susan's favorite room.

For her senior project, Susan put together a book of photographs about being behind the scenes at the White House.

The Carters

Where the president's children should go to school is a big question for first families with school-age kids. Amy Carter was 9 years old and in the third grade when she moved to Washington from Georgia. Her father, Jimmy Carter, was elected president in 1976. Her parents decided to send Amy to public school in Washington.

Amy was the youngest of four Carter children. The other three were grown when the family moved into the White House. Two sons and their wives lived in the White House, too.

Amy with her cat, Misty Malarky Ying Yang.

© Charles M. Rafshoon

Meeting important people is one of the treats of being a "first kid." Important people enjoy meeting the president's son or daughter, so helping greet people becomes a duty.

Jimmy Carter Presidential Library

Amy was included in many grown-up White House dinners. Here, Amy's dad introduces her to the president of Mexico.

White House Photo

Amy helps her mom greet guests at a special party for kids.

White House Collection

Amy Carter's father was governor of Georgia before he became president. He also had been a peanut farmer and a naval officer. Presidents have had many jobs before going into office: U.S. congressman, senator, lawyer, newspaper editor, professor and even movie actor.

Amy Carter sits in her dad's lap and blows a bubble.

Scout's
White House Families
Word Search

Words that remind us of families in the White House are hidden in the block below. Some words are hidden backward. See if you can find: WHITE, HOUSE, FLOOR, SECOND, THIRD, FIRST, PETS, SCHOOLING, FATHER, GRANDDAUGHTER, GRANDSON, DAUGHTER, SON, PRESIDENT, HOME, KIDS, EVENTS, OFFICE, HOST.

IT'S FUN TO LIVE IN THE WHITE HOUSE!

```
R E T H G U A D D N A R G S S
G A J X D A U G H T E R P O C
R B F A T H E R E S U O H N H
A F T N E D I S E R P C K O O
N L H O S T D W H I T E K F O
D O F P E T S D R I H T I F L
S O G S T N E V E M Q T D I I
O R N D N O C E S U H N S C N
N I F I R S T A C F H O M E G
```

Amy Carter with her nephew in her tree house on the South Lawn.

Mrs. Carter listens as Amy practices her violin.

A special tree house was built for Amy Carter on the White House South Lawn. Amy and her father designed it. It was a wonderful private place for a little girl who had been in the spotlight most of her life.

The Clintons

Chelsea Clinton's move at the age of 12 from Little Rock, Ark., meant adjusting to a new city and a new school.

Her father became president in 1993.

While she had always gone to public schools in Arkansas, the Clintons decided to send her to a private school in Washington. They go out of their way to protect her privacy.

Chelsea Clinton and Socks visited her father in the Oval Office in 1994. This was on Christmas Eve, just before Chelsea and her father made a last-minute trip to a nearby shopping mall.

Like Amy Carter's, Chelsea Clinton's family had been in the spotlight most of her life. She, too, had been brought up in a governor's mansion. Her father had been governor of Arkansas for five two-year terms.

President Clinton and Chelsea.

President and Mrs. Clinton plant a tree on the South Lawn. For many years, presidents have planted commemorative trees on the White House lawn. The gold-plated shovels they use are for very special occasions. Nailed on them are metal labels marking the date and kind of tree the president or first lady planted.

Scout's
White House
Puzzle-le-do

Fit the names of these things you might find in the Oval Office into the puzzle.

ACROSS:

1.

3.

5.

6.

7.

DOWN:

1.

2.

4.

Across: 1. picture, 3. flag, 5. plant, 6. clock, 7. desk. Down: 1. pen, 2. telephone, 4. couch.

Chelsea and her mother are very close friends.

Chelsea, her mother and father take a walk on the South Lawn just before taking a trip to Europe in 1994.

The state of Virginia, with eight presidents born there, is known as the "mother of presidents." Ohio is second, with seven presidents who were born there.

Virginia presidents: Washington, Jefferson, Madison, Monroe, William Henry Harrison, Tyler, Taylor, Wilson. Ohio presidents: Grant, Hayes, Garfield, Benjamin Harrison, McKinley, Taft, Harding.

First Ladies

From Martha Washington on, the role of the first lady has been important. Mrs. Washington described herself as "an old-fashioned housekeeper." However, first ladies are much more than that.

What a first lady does and what we think of her are important to her husband's success.

Abigail Adams, wife of John Adams, was the first president's wife to move into the White House. She was well-informed and often gave her husband her views on matters. Her enemies often called her "Mrs. President."

"Remember the ladies," she wrote her husband when he was in Philadelphia at the time the Declaration of Independence was adopted.

White House Collection

Although Martha Washington never lived in the White House, her portrait hangs in the East Room.

courtesy Board of Trustees, National Gallery of Art, Washington, D.C.

Abigail Adams

Only two first ladies have also been the mothers of presidents.

Abigail Adams was the wife of the second president, John Adams, and the mother of the seventh president John Quincy Adams. Barbara Bush is the wife of the 41st President, George Bush, and the mother of the 43rd President, George W. Bush.

White House Collection

Barbara Bush

There is no description for the first lady's job. Each first lady decides the best way to handle this difficult, full-time, non-paying job. The role a first lady plays depends on the needs of her husband, the customs of the times and her own personality.

The customs

It used to be that first ladies were expected to pay social calls, or visits, on wives of important people in Washington. Most of the early first ladies spent much time in their carriage traveling to such official visits.

The needs of her husband

Eleanor Roosevelt had to meet the special needs of her husband. President Franklin Roosevelt was badly disabled by polio. It was difficult for him to travel.

She helped him by traveling on his behalf in this country and around the world. She would report back what she saw and heard.

Eleanor Roosevelt

Her personality

Mary Todd Lincoln spent a lot of money on White House furnishings, her clothes and parties. She felt that she had to impress Washington society because she was from the "frontier" state of Illinois.

Mary Todd Lincoln

President James Buchanan was the only president who never married. His niece, Harriet Lane, served as his hostess.

Harriet Lane's portrait was done many years after she served as hostess and first lady.

35

The First Ladies' Roles

The first lady has a lot of work to do when her husband is president. She must decide how to handle her role as ...

Betty Ford poses with her husband and family.

• **a wife and mother.**

Some first ladies have to balance their roles of wife and mother with many other duties.

Edith Wilson often assisted her husband in many routine duties.

• **an adviser to her husband.**

Many presidents rely on their wives for advice and ideas.

Eleanor Roosevelt volunteered for many worthy causes.

Eleanor Roosevelt set an example for the first ladies who followed. No other first lady had been so interested and outspoken on so many causes. She was the first to hold press conferences. She traveled a great deal and wrote a newspaper column.

Barbara Bush was very interested in literacy and encouraged reading.

• **a worker for a cause.**

A first lady often chooses to do a special project while she is in the White House.

Nancy Reagan appears before the press to present an award to an outstanding teacher.

• **a messenger to the people.**

First ladies must know how to use the press to reach the people with their message and the impression they want to make.

President and Mrs. Clinton welcome the president of South Korea and his wife for a state dinner in July 1995.

• **a hostess.**

A first lady must give many large dinners, parties and entertainments throughout the year.

Jacqueline Kennedy's special interest was restoring the White House.

• **a worker to preserve history and art.**

Some first ladies have been especially interested in this country's music, theater, art, buildings and dance.

Frances Cleveland was the youngest presidential wife. She was only 21 years old when she married Grover Cleveland in the White House.

First Pets

Most visitors do not see the first pets. These kids got a special treat. Socks appeared on the grand staircase.

President Bill Clinton with Socks.

Rounding out the presidential family are the presidential pets. Most presidents have at least one.

Being a part of the first family makes them special. They get a lot of attention. They are pampered and loved, not only by the first families, but also by the public.

Some people are almost as thrilled over seeing the "first pet" as they are at seeing the president!

First pets are in great demand. "I wish we had seven Socks," said a member of Bill Clinton's staff. Socks, the Clinton family cat, was very popular.

The family of current president George W. Bush includes two dogs, Spot and Barney, and a cat named India.

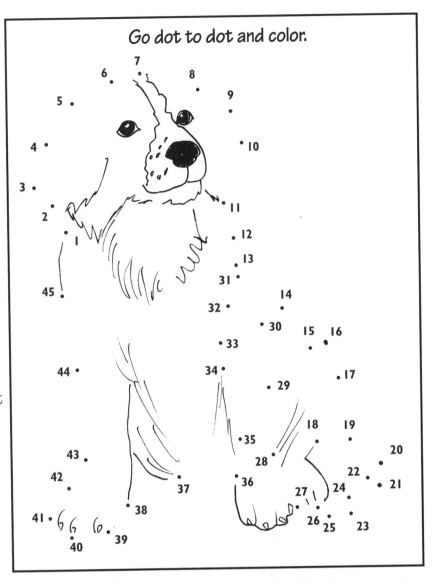

Go dot to dot and color.

President Bush's dog, Spot, is an English springer spaniel. She is the daughter of former President George Bush's dog, Millie. She was born in the White House on March 17, 1989, and is the only second-generation presidential pet in history. She likes dry dog food and sleeps on a chair in the First Couple's bedroom.

Barney, a Scottish terrier, is said to be unusually well-behaved for a puppy. Currently he sleeps in a crate in the upstairs kitchen. Once he's housebroken, he may graduate to a sleeping spot in the First Couple's bedroom. Barney likes dry dog food as well.

No one else lives in the White House except the president, his family and their pets. There are uniformed Secret Service officers and also those who are not in uniform on duty 24 hours a day.

First Pets and the Presidents

President George Bush with the springer spaniel Millie and her puppies on the South Lawn.

First pets can sleep anywhere in the White House the first family wishes. However, most are not often allowed in the public rooms.

The Bush family's dogs lived in the first family's rooms upstairs. Mrs. Bush would take them outside each morning for a walk. Usually members of the White House staff help care for and walk the pets. Some dogs have lived in dog houses on the South Lawn.

Susan Ford said that her father took Liberty, the Ford family dog, with him to the Oval Office. But Liberty "didn't sleep upstairs. She was put in a kennel at night because it's a long way down the elevator and out the door."

President Lyndon Johnson was especially fond of his mutt Yuki. His daughter Luci found Yuki at a gas station in Texas. Yuki and the president sometimes sang together.

In 1972, President Nixon and the American people were given two giant pandas from China. They were sent to the National Zoo.

40

President Woodrow Wilson kept sheep on the South Lawn during World War I. They kept the grass cropped short while the White House gardeners were off serving their country.

Abby's
White House Pets
Word Search

Names of animals that have lived in the White House are hidden in the block below. Some words are hidden backward or diagonally. See if you can find: ALLIGATOR, BADGER, BIRD, OWL, PARROT, CAT, COW, DEER, DOG, DONKEY, GOAT, GUINEA PIG, HAMSTER, HORSE, LAMB, SHEEP, FISH, SQUIRREL, RABBIT, RAT, RACCOON.

DO YOU KNOW WHO THIS IS?

```
A L L I G A T O R H D E E R B
C M W C A T D G H K O G O A T
D N O O C C A R N B O R Y F L
D F P E E H S O R I A W S Z A
O H A M S T E R G A Q D L E M
N B I R D H R C O W B F G C B
K S Q U I R R E L J D B I E T
E K T A R T O R R A P O I S R
Y L V G I P A E N I U G G T H
```

President Franklin Roosevelt's dog, Fala, went everywhere with him. Fala was perhaps the most famous of all presidential pets.

THE PRESIDENT WAS NOT PLEASED.

Fala, the famous Scottie, once traveled with the president aboard a Navy ship. Fala disappeared for a while. When he returned, a lot of his hair was missing. Sailors had snipped it off for souvenirs!

First Pets and First Ladies

Of all the first families, Calvin Coolidge and his wife, Grace, had the most pets. Their fondness for animals was so well-known that people even sent them pets that they no longer wanted. Some of the wilder ones went to the zoo.

The pets they kept included dogs, cats, raccoons, donkeys and birds.

First lady Grace Coolidge with her pet raccoon, Rebecca. President Coolidge was very fond of Rebecca, too. He used to take her for walks around the White House on a leash.

$400,000

Library of Congress

White House Collection

Grace Coolidge's portrait includes her collie, Rob Roy.

1921 World's Work

President and Mrs. Warren Harding had an Airedale named Laddie Boy. Here, first lady Florence Harding shakes Laddie Boy's paw. The Hardings once gave Laddie Boy a birthday party and invited all the neighborhood dogs.

Paw prints of first pets are always popular. Here are prints from Millie Bush and her puppies.

Nancy Reagan's dog, Rex.

Nancy Reagan had a King Charles spaniel named Rex. Rex stayed in the family quarters on the second floor.

Barbara Bush's portrait includes her springer spaniel, Millie.

Rex rushes to meet the Reagans after their helicopter lands on the South Lawn.

There have been some very famous first pets. First lady Barbara Bush wrote a book about life in the White House from her dog Millie's point of view. It was a best seller.

A History of Visitors

Only a few months after the first president moved in, John Adams held the first public reception on Jan. 1, 1801. The New Year's reception became a custom that lasted more than 130 years. After shaking hands with a total of 6,000 guests in a few hours for three New Year's Eve receptions in a row, President Herbert Hoover and his wife stopped the custom in 1933.

Perley's Reminiscences

At a New Year's Day reception in 1866, President Andrew Johnson receives guests as they stream through the receiving line.

A drawing of a crowd attending one of Jackson's popular receptions.

White House Collection

At an inaugural party in 1829, Andrew Jackson invited his supporters to come help celebrate. About 10,000 people did. The new president had to leave through a window and spend the night at a nearby hotel.

In the years that followed, the White House was often crowded with visitors.

Andrew Jackson was so tough that he was called "Old Hickory." Hickory is a type of wood that is very hard. A magnolia tree that Jackson planted in memory of his wife is still growing on the South Lawn.

White House Collection

Amelia Earhart, the famous pilot, was awarded a medal by President Herbert Hoover.

White-frocked girls dance around a maypole during Hoover's presidency.

Acme, June 21, 1932

Library of Congress

Pope John Paul II visited the White House as a guest of President and Mrs. Carter in 1979.

Donald J. Crump, National Geographic Society

Sometimes children of diplomats are invited to a Christmas party at the White House.

White House Photo

Perley's Reminiscences

President Andrew Jackson held another party after receiving a huge 1,400-pound chunk of cheese. Guests dropped crumbs that were trod into rugs. The White House smelled of cheese for weeks.

Your White House

The White House from this view overlooks a big back yard.

The White House that George Washington helped build is the most famous house in the world. To visit there fills everyone with a sense of pride and awe.

For more than 200 years, the White House has been a special place for Americans. It's an unusual house that belongs to all U.S. citizens.

The White House serves many purposes. It is:

• a **home** for the president and his family.

• an **office** for the president and the people who work for him.

• a **museum.** The White House owns many historic, precious and famous objects. People come from all over the country and the world to see them. It is the scene of more events in U.S. history than any other place.

The public has been welcomed ever since the first president to live there, John Adams, moved in, in 1800. Each year, more than a million people visit the White House.

• a **symbol** that the leadership of the United States can pass from one president to another in a peaceful way. Every four years, voters decide who will live here.

The seal of the president of the United States. At one time the eagle faced the arrows. President Truman changed it to face the olive branch, a symbol of peace. The presidential seal can be found on flags, walls and even on the Oval Office rug.

After living in the White House for eight years, President and Mrs. Eisenhower say goodbye to the White House staff.

The incoming president, John Kennedy, Jacqueline Kennedy, Caroline and baby John Jr. were the next family to live there.

The White House is open on a regular basis, free of charge. No other home of a leader of a country is so open to the public.

Welcome!

The People in the Portraits

Because it has been used for more than 200 years, the White House is filled with the history of the United States, its presidents and their families.

There is an interesting person behind each of the many portraits you will see.

Write the room in which you see the following portraits. They are in the rooms pictured in this book and on the tour.

all White House Collection

Thomas Jefferson was the third president, but the second president to live in the White House.

1.

George Washington could be called the "father of the White House," too.

2.

Dolley Madison was the wife of President James Madison and a famous hostess.

3.

Abraham Lincoln was a great leader during the Civil War.

4.

James Madison was our fourth president. He was president when the White House burned.

5.

The Cutaway

This inside view of the White House is called a "cutaway." It will give you an idea of which rooms you will visit on your tour.

People on the public tour visit the ground floor hall. Then they go upstairs and visit the "state," or public, rooms. Tourists, of course, are not allowed to sit on the furniture and cannot go into the family living quarters on the second floor.

Robert W. Nicholson, National Geographic Society

The rooms that are open to the public are starred. We have also numbered them here and in the next pages.

Ground Floor

1. **Colonnade and East Wing*** (Visitors enter here.)
2. **Ground floor corridor***
3. **Library**
4. **Vermeil Room**
5. **China Room**
6. **Diplomatic Reception Room**

Main Floor

7. **East Room***
8. **Green Room***
9. **Blue Room***
10. **Red Room***
11. **State Dining Room***
12. **Cross Hall***
13. **Entrance Hall***
14. **South Portico**

49

1. The Colonnade

To get to the main building of the White House, tourists walk down a long hall with windows on one side. This is called a "colonnade." The guides are members of the Secret Service Uniform Division.

Out of the colonnade's windows you will see the Jacqueline Kennedy Garden (often called the East Garden) and the South Lawn.

The colonnade leads to …

2. The Ground Floor Corridor

This hall is the main passageway up to the public rooms on the floor above. At one time, this was a basement used as work space. There are two basements under this one.

Portraits of many first ladies are hung here and in nearby rooms. A painting of Barbara Bush, wife of President George Bush, hangs on one of the walls.

Thomas Jefferson, our third president, added the colonnades to the White House. His is one of the busts of famous Americans on display.

On the ground floor you may be able to peek into several of the rooms that aren't on the public tour.

3. Library

Most of the books in this room were written and illustrated by American authors or are about American subjects.

4. Vermeil Room

Vermeil is silver covered with gold. The White House has a good collection of it.

5. China Room

Many presidents had sets of china made for the White House. The White House has some of the china on display in this room.

6. The Diplomatic Reception Room

The first family often enters and leaves the White House through this room. It has historical wallpaper showing views of North America in the 1800s.

51

7. The East Room

President Clinton holds a press conference in the East Room because it is so big.

The East Room is the largest room in the White House. It has been used for weddings, dances, dinners, receptions, concerts, funerals, church services, press conferences, bill-signing ceremonies and many other events.

The East Room usually has very little furniture since it is used for large gatherings.

President Garfield's sons rode their three-wheel bikes in this room while having a pillow fight.

The East Room has also seen some unusual events. Union troops briefly occupied the room during the Civil War. Theodore Roosevelt held boxing matches here.

This portrait of George Washington is the one item that has been in the White House since it was built, so it is a great treasure.

The Green Room, Blue Room and Red Room are used for receptions and small meetings. Most of the furnishings are examples of fine American furniture made by master craftsmen.

These rooms got their names from the colors they have been decorated in over the years.

8. The Green Room

Thomas Jefferson used this room as a dining room. It has been used as a bedroom, dining room, card room and parlor.

The guides answer questions as tourists walk through on the self-guided tours. When the tours are over, the ropes come down and the rugs are unrolled. Then the room is ready for entertaining.

The silver coffee urn was used by President John Adams. The candlesticks belonged to James Madison and James Monroe. The painting on the wall is of Independence Hall in Philadelphia.

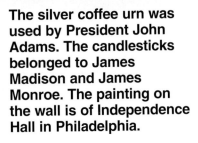

After the morning tours are over, guests invited to special events are allowed to sit in the chairs. Notice that a portrait of Benjamin Franklin hangs over the fireplace.

53

9. The Blue Room

Many people consider the Blue Room to be the most beautiful room in the White House. The only president ever to get married in the White House, Grover Cleveland, was married here.

A guide points out the room's oval shape. There are three oval rooms in the original White House, one on top of the other.

President and Mrs. Clinton in front of the traditional White House Christmas tree.

From the windows there is a beautiful view of the South Lawn, the Washington Monument and the Jefferson Memorial.

An afternoon guest sits between a portrait of James Madison (left) and Thomas Jefferson (right). Some of the original furniture that James Monroe bought after the fire of 1814 is in this room.

10. The Red Room

Like many rooms in the White House, this one has been used in many ways.

It was a yellow reception room during Dolley Madison's day.

Today it is used for small gatherings.

Dolley Madison's portrait hangs in the Red Room. The popular wife of James Madison was a famous Washington hostess.

White House Collection

© Bill Petros

Because of the large number of tours, visitors cannot sit on sofas. However, after the tours are over, invited guests may enjoy this treat. This guest sits on a sofa that is a fine example of American furniture. The dolphin feet are unusual.

White House Historical Association

A bust of President Martin Van Buren is up high. Can you find it in a painting of his daughter-in-law, Abigail Singleton Van Buren?

© Bill Fitz-Patrick

A guide points out a small round table that is old and has an unusual design.

11. State Dining Room

The State Dining Room used to be smaller than it is now. Thomas Jefferson used it as an office. It has also served as a Cabinet room.

Today the room is used for big dinners, receptions and meetings.

A portrait of Abraham Lincoln hangs over the fireplace. It was painted four years after Lincoln's death.

White House Collection

White House Historical Association

To be invited to a big dinner at the White House is an honor. As many as 140 people can be served.

© Bill Fitz-Patrick

Although across the room and somewhat hard to see, there are buffalo heads carved in the marble mantel. These used to be lions' heads until President Theodore Roosevelt had them changed.

Carved below the mantel are the words John Adams wrote in a letter during his second night at the White House:

"I Pray Heaven to Bestow the Best of Blessings on THIS HOUSE and on all that shall hereafter Inhabit it. May none but Honest and Wise Men ever rule under this roof."

© Bill Petros

The beautiful gold centerpiece and its fruit baskets on the long dining table are nearly 200 years old. They are some of the most valuable White House treasures.

12. The Cross Hall

The Cross Hall stretches from the East Room to the State Dining Room. The Red, Blue and Green Rooms are connected to it.

The presidential seal is set in the wall above the door to the Blue Room. The president's flag and the United States flag are along the wall.

13. The Entrance Hall

The Entrance Hall is seen by visitors as they end the tour.

The view out of the north door is of Pennsylvania Avenue and Lafayette Park across the street.

The Grand Staircase is used for very special occasions. The seals of the original 13 states are set in the entrance hall floor.

1817
President Monroe moves in after the fire.

1792
House building started.

1902
First floor renovated and West Wing added.

1952
Truman moves in after the restoration.

A special stone in the hall floor is set with important dates in the history of the White House.

The Big Back Yard

While tour groups do not go on the South Lawn, or the "big back yard," we asked these boys and girls to show you some things first families and their guests might enjoy. We have numbered where these pictures were taken.

1. Children relaxing in the Children's Garden, a special spot created by Lady Bird Johnson. Visitors can also compare their handprints with those of some presidents' grandchildren.

© Bill Fitz-Patrick

4. Guests sitting by the pool.

© Bill Petros

5. Visitors standing on the tennis court.

2. Kids play basketball.

© Bill Fitz-Patrick

3. A guest gazes at the fountain.

© Bill Petros

58

6. A group walks down the West Colonnade on the way to the Oval Office.

7. Two girls admire the flowers and trees in the Rose Garden.

8. Guests using the putting green.

9. A jogger runs on the jogging path.

J. E. Barrett (illustration)

WE HAVE ALSO NUMBERED SOME OTHER PARTS OF THE WHITE HOUSE:

10. The East Wing (Visitors Entrance)
11. The East Colonnade
12. Jacqueline Kennedy Garden
13. South Portico
14. North Portico
15. Oval Office
16. West Wing

59

The Busy, Big Back Yard

The South Lawn serves many purposes.

Helicopter landings: The president's helicopter lands close to the White House.

White House Photo

White House Photo

Arrival ceremonies: When leaders from other countries come to visit, they are honored at a colorful outdoor ceremony. At this ceremony, President Clinton welcomes the president of Italy.

The South Portico faces the big back yard.

Easter Egg Rolls: On each Easter Monday there is a big event for children ages 3 to 7. Above, the Easter Bunny greets two of President George Bush's grandchildren. Singers, storytellers, performers and volunteers entertain thousands of kids and the adults they bring along.

Outdoor meetings: Presidents often use the Rose Garden as an outdoor meeting place. President Clinton greets a group of hockey stars. For big events, tents are put up.

Gardening: The director of the White House grounds and gardens points out the oldest tree on the White House lawn. It was planted by President Andrew Jackson.

The Oval Office

Beside the Rose Garden is the Oval Office where the president works. Presidents may decorate it any way they wish. They may add photographs and other personal items.

Presidents use the Oval Office to work in, meet visitors and hold important meetings. It is a very powerful room that impresses everyone who enters.

Most presidents also have a nearby office and another office on the second floor in the family living quarters.

White House Historical Association

President Bill Clinton's desk in the Oval Office.

© Bill Fitz-Patrick

This photo shows the view past President Clinton's desk. These young visitors are examining the presidential seal that is woven into the rug.

The Cabinet Room

Each president has a group of special people who help him run the executive branch of the government. The top people in each government agency make up the "President's Cabinet." Most of them are called secretaries.

The president usually sits in the middle of the table. The vice president generally sits across from him.

The Cabinet Room is near the Oval Office.

President George Bush meets with his Cabinet.

All Cabinet members have their names on the back of their special chairs.

THE SECRETARY WILL LIKE THIS!

When Cabinet members leave their jobs, they take their chair with them. Their staff usually pays for it and presents it to them as a gift and souvenir.

63

The Second Floor

No tours are permitted in the upstairs rooms. But if you know the president or a member of his family, you might be lucky enough to be invited up.

The Lincoln Bedroom

The Lincoln Bedroom is one of 10 bedrooms on the second and third floors. It served as Lincoln's office when he was president.

© Bill Fitz-Patrick

A visitor examines a signed copy of the Gettysburg Address that is on display. Lincoln delivered this speech in 1863 when he dedicated a national cemetery in Gettysburg, Pa. In this room, Lincoln signed the Emancipation Proclamation, also in 1863.

© Bill Fitz-Patrick

While Lincoln probably never slept in this bed, other presidents have, including Theodore Roosevelt and Woodrow Wilson.

The Yellow Oval Room

The president and first lady use this room on very formal occasions when they have important guests.

The first president to live in the White House, John Adams, held the first reception in this room in 1801.

In the past, presidents and their families have used the room as a library, a family living room, an office and a study.

The room also leads to the Truman Balcony.

White House Historical Association

The president and first lady often entertain important leaders from other countries in this beautiful room.

Seeing the President

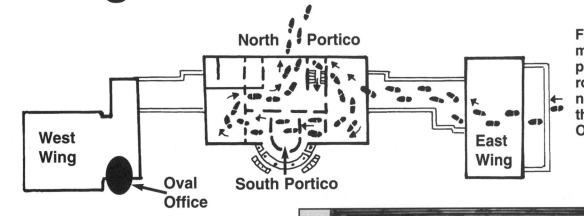

North Portico

Footprints mark the public tour route. It does not go near the Oval Office.

West Wing

East Wing

Oval Office

South Portico

"Are we going to see the president?" visitors on the tours sometimes ask.

Although presidents have been known to greet tour groups, they usually are very busy. The Oval Office is not on your tour.

You must have an appointment. Before the president sees you, he is given a sheet of paper by his staff that says who you are and why you are there. He also has discussed your visit with his staff.

Visitors who are going to meet with the president wait in a reception room in the West Wing. Notice the painting of "Washington Crossing the Delaware."

BE ON TIME.

Before meeting the president, or on any visit to the White House when you are not part of a tour, you must give your full name and furnish certain information. This enables the Secret Service to do a background check of you.

Write your birthday here.

Adults have to give Social Security numbers. Do you have one? If so, write it here.

The Branches of Government

The White House is a powerful place because it is the home of our president, the chief executive of the United States.

To find out why it is such a powerful place, we have to look at the U.S. Constitution.

The Constitution begins with the famous words, "We the people ..."

The Constitution is the single most important document we have as a nation. The writers who created it in 1787 divided it into parts called "articles."

They wanted a strong national government. But they did not want to give too much power to one person or one group of people.

They decided that the powers should be divided into three "branches," or parts. This idea is called "the separation of powers."

Here are the branches of government, the people who work in them and their powers. We have also listed the section or article in the Constitution where these powers are found.

We often use buildings in Washington, D.C., to represent these branches.

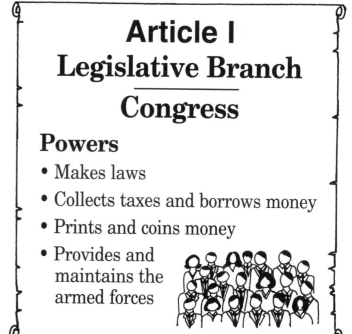

Article I
Legislative Branch

Congress

Powers

- Makes laws
- Collects taxes and borrows money
- Prints and coins money
- Provides and maintains the armed forces

1. The U.S. Capitol building is where our Congress meets.

2. The White House, where our president lives and works.

Article II
Executive Branch
The President

Powers

- Sees that laws are carried out
- Heads the armed forces
- Appoints people to jobs
- Makes treaties
- Signs or vetoes laws

White House Historical Association

Article III
Judicial Branch
The Supreme Court and other national courts

Powers

- Explains the meanings of the laws
- Decides whether laws passed by Congress are in keeping with the Constitution

Supreme Court of the United States

3. The Supreme Court justices meet in this building.

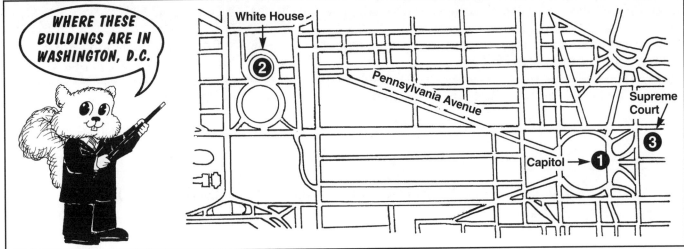

WHERE THESE BUILDINGS ARE IN WASHINGTON, D.C.

White House

Pennsylvania Avenue

Supreme Court

Capitol

67

The President Has Many Jobs

The White House is a stage for most of what the president does. The president has many jobs:

- as **chief executive officer**, he must propose laws he thinks should be passed.
- as **economic leader**, he must try to keep our businesses busy and our workers on the job.
- as **chief diplomat**, he helps decide how our country will act toward other countries.
- as **chief of state**, he represents our country here and in other lands.
- as **commander in chief**, the president is in charge of the armed forces.
- as **party leader**, he has a lot of influence over the way his political party thinks about our national problems.

President Jimmy Carter used the North Grounds as a setting for the signing of a peace agreement between Egypt and Israel.

Presidents must be sworn into office on Jan. 20 of an inaugural year. If this is on a Sunday, an informal ceremony is held. The official one takes place the next day. President Ronald Reagan took the oath of office in an informal ceremony in the White House on the Grand Staircase on Sunday, Jan. 20, 1985.

President Gerald Ford uses the Rose Garden for a meeting with the press.

The oath of office that all presidents take is in the Constitution.

"I do solemnly swear (or affirm) that I will faithfully execute the office of the president of the United States, and will to the best of my ability, preserve, protect and defend the Constitution of the United States."

President Lyndon Johnson signing the Civil Rights Act of 1964.

Lyndon Johnson signed the Civil Rights Act of 1964 at the White House. It was a bill dealing with equal rights. One of the president's jobs is to propose laws that he thinks should be passed.

Notice the pens on the table. Before a bill becomes law, the president must sign it. Sometimes presidents use many pens to sign one bill. They give these pens to special people who have worked to get the bill through Congress.

To do: Get several pencils or pens. Sign your name using different pencils for each part. Can you make it take as many as 20 different strokes?

_____

What law would you want the president to sign?

"The greatest part of the president's job is to make decisions ... big ones and small ones, dozens of them every day. He can't pass the buck to anyone. No one else can do the deciding for him. That's his job."
President Harry S. Truman

A Country Is Coming

When a leader from another country comes to visit, we call the event a "state visit." The president and the White House go all out to make a nice impression.

The purpose of these visits is not just to entertain, but for the leaders from two countries to sit down and discuss important matters.

President and Mrs. Clinton greet the arriving guests. In this case, the president of Italy, Oscar Luigi Scalfaro, was visiting with his daughter in 1996.

all photos this page from the White House

The arrival ceremony

A state visit usually begins with an arrival ceremony on the South Lawn. Every branch of the armed forces is represented.

- Bands play. Members of the military march.
- The president and visitor review the troops.
- The president gives an official welcome.
- The visiting leader responds.

Along with a ceremonial officer, President Clinton and President Scalfaro inspect the troops.

The arrival ceremony was started by President John Kennedy. It usually takes about 25 minutes.

There is usually a big state dinner held that night. Some young visitors got a chance to go behind the scenes as the White House prepared for one.

It is a great honor to get an invitation. A calligrapher (a skilled person with beautiful handwriting) helps address each invitation. Calligraphers also designed the menu below. Can you read it?

© Bill Petros

The White House has a florist in the basement. Fresh flowers are always placed throughout the house. The flowers for state dinner tables are approved by the first lady.

DINNER

Honoring His Excellency
Oscar Luigi Scalfaro
President of the Italian Republic

Chilled Spring Pea and Zucchini Soup
Herb Marinated Young Vegetables
Lamb Loin with Basil Polenta,
Portabello Mushroom, Roasted Peppers & Fava Bean Ragout
Barolo Sauce

Young Lettuces and Sprouts
Layered Asiago and Goat's Cheese
Rhubarb Dressing

Strawberry Surprise
Lemon Burned Cream
Almond Pistachio Nougat
Chestnut Gondola

White House Photo

At the state dinner, the president welcomes the visitor with words of praise for the country and its leaders. The guest responds.

State dinners usually have four courses: an appetizer, a main dish, a salad and a dessert. There are as many as 28 items for one place setting.

Music at the White House

Music is an important part of all White House events. When John and Abigail Adams held the first New Year's reception at the White House, they asked the Marine Band to play. The Marine Band plays at the White House on many occasions. While bands from other branches of the service are also asked to perform, the Marine Band is called "The President's Own." John Philip Sousa, the famous march king, led this band for many years.

White House Photo

The Marine Band plays dance music in the East Room after a dinner. Band members also play marches at ceremonies or background music at receptions.

White House Collection

President James Polk was a small man. When he walked into a crowded room, people could not see him. His wife had the idea of announcing his arrival with a special tune, "Hail to the Chief." It became the president's official entrance music.

Presidents often ask singers, dancers or musicians to perform at the White House. It is a great honor, and performers are not paid. Entertainers are pleased to accept the president's invitation.

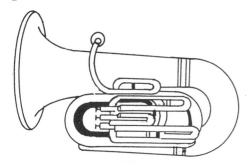

The famous performer Eubie Blake plays a piano at a jazz festival on the South Lawn.

Donald J. Crump, National Geographic Society

White House Photo

Native American dancers from New Mexico furnish the entertainment in the East Room after a White House dinner.

Scout's Music Scramble

Unscramble the names of these musical instruments.

1. lbegu   _ _ _ _ _

2. tleuf   _ _ _ _ _

3. oniliv   _ _ _ _ _ _

4. srmud   _ _ _ _ _

5. mrneootb   _ _ _ _ _ _ _ _

Answers: 1. bugle, 2. flute, 3. violin, 4. drums, 5. trombone.

Some presidents are musicians themselves. Harry Truman and Richard Nixon were two who played the piano. Bill Clinton plays the saxophone.

Technology

While some traditions like the Marine Band have been around for a long time, the White House is usually among the first to get new improvements to make working and living easier. Today the White House has computers, satellite dishes and the latest in technology.

Gordon Phillips

In 1800, when the Adamses moved in, nobody (not even the president of the United States) had indoor plumbing. Washing clothes was quite a chore. Water was taken from wells on the grounds. Later rainwater was collected from big buckets on the roof.

By the year 1833, the White House had running water.

Since the president's family did not want to hang the laundry out for all to see, the East Room proved to be the perfect spot for it.

© Photos Culver

Some presidents have special needs. Four workers could sit in a huge tub installed just for William Howard Taft. He went into office in 1909.

White House Collection

At more than 300 pounds, William Howard Taft was our heaviest president. He is the only president to later become chief justice of the United States.

74

Robert W. Nicholson

By candlelight, Franklin Pierce leads one of his assistants up the White House stairs. Gas lighting was installed in 1848. Electricity was installed in 1891. At first, people were afraid to turn it on because they might get shocked.

Abby's Technology Word Search

Words that remind us of technology in the White House are hidden in the block below. Some are hidden backward. See if you can find: RADIO, TELEPHONE, COMPUTER, WIRES, SATELLITE, TELEGRAPH, MACHINERY, TRANSMIT, KEYBOARD, AUTOMATED, INVENTION, POWER, FAX, COPIER, PRINTER, TOOLS.

THE WHITE HOUSE HAS ALL THE LATEST TECHNOLOGY!

```
T E T I L L E T A S B T T M K
E C T R A N S M I T C O E A E
L P R I N T E R E E O O L C Y
E F M G C O P I E R M L E H B
P H R E W O P X A F P S G I O
H A U T O M A T E D U H R N A
O N O I T N E V N I T J A E R
N K R A D I O O Q T E V P R D
E S E R I W L P R U R W H Y X
```

Kenneth Garrett

In 1969, Richard Nixon called astronauts on the moon. This photo shows Nixon (in the upper left) talking to astronauts Neil Armstrong and Buzz Aldrin, the first men to land there.

THE PHONE NUMBER WAS 1.

When the first telephone was installed in the White House in 1879, there was almost nobody to call. Few people had phones.

On the Way to the Oval Office

Someday, some boy or girl reading this book or visiting the White House might grow up to become president of the United States and live and work in the White House.

It is interesting to see how presidents decorate the Oval Office. These are official office photos. While presidents do have other desks they use, they are not always this neat.

President Lyndon Johnson's Oval Office

President George Bush's Oval Office

White House Historical Association

White House Collection

The Oval Office and the West Wing were added about 100 years after the main White House was built. The oval shape copies that of the Blue Room.

President
Jimmy Carter's
Oval Office

White House Historical Association

White House Collection

President
Ronald
Reagan's Oval
Office

White House Historical Association

White House Collection

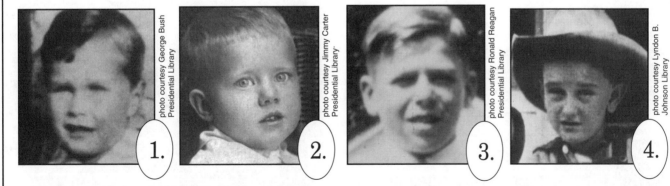

Can you match these presidential growing-up photos with the grown-up ones?

photo courtesy George Bush Presidential Library

1.

photo courtesy Jimmy Carter Presidential Library

2.

photo courtesy Ronald Reagan Presidential Library

3.

photo courtesy Lyndon B. Johnson Library

4.

Answers: 1. George Bush, 2. Jimmy Carter, 3. Ronald Reagan, 4. Lyndon Johnson

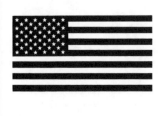

When presidents leave office, they take the flags with them. On the left is the U.S. flag. On the right is the flag with the presidential seal.

White House Q and A

We asked kids from across the country to tell us what they wanted to know about the White House. We asked the White House experts, Scout and Abby, to help answer these questions for us.

Ghosts

Q. Does the White House have ghosts?

A. Most of us really don't believe in ghosts. But we all like ghost stories.

The most famous White House ghost is Abraham Lincoln. About 40 years after Lincoln's death, Theodore Roosevelt said he often saw Lincoln's ghost. Presidents, their wives and White House workers have sensed his presence.

Lincoln's wife, Mary Todd Lincoln, was interested in the supernatural. She sometimes held seances, or meetings, with people who claimed they could put her in touch with departed loved ones.

Exercise

Q. Is there an exercise room in the White House?

A. Yes, there is one on the third floor. It is right down the hall from the solarium, or "family room."

It is important that presidents keep in shape. President Ford liked to swim. He had a new swimming pool built on the South Lawn. Friends of the president raised money to pay for it.

The White House used to have an indoor pool along the colonnade leading to the West Wing. Children helped raise money to build one for Franklin Roosevelt. President Nixon removed the pool and changed the area into a press room for photographers and reporters covering the president.

White House Photo

As members of the press watch, President Gerald Ford swims in the new White House pool.

78

Weddings

Q. Has there ever been a wedding in the White House?

A. There have been many weddings in the White House.

President Grover Cleveland shakes the hand of a well-wisher as his bride kisses her mother. Cleveland is the only president to marry in the White House. They were married in 1886.

Lynda Johnson Robb and Charles Robb walk under the swords held by Marines after their marriage in the East Room in 1967. Lynda Johnson is the daughter of Lyndon Johnson.

Tricia Nixon Cox and Edward Cox were the first to be married outdoors at the White House. They were married in the Rose Garden in 1971. Tricia Nixon is the daughter of Richard Nixon.

Demonstrations

This demonstrator was trying to convince President Woodrow Wilson that women should be allowed to vote.

Q. Is it legal to demonstrate in front of the White House?

A. Yes. Over the years, people have tried to get the president's attention by carrying signs and parading and sometimes yelling and chanting their views. However, demonstrators must have a permit from the National Park Service.

A group, carrying signs and chanting, marches in front of the White House in 1996.

79

President Eisenhower escorts President-elect Kennedy from the White House to the Capitol for the swearing-in ceremony.

President and Mrs. Carter and Amy walk down Pennsylvania Avenue on the way to the White House.

Moving in

Q. How do first families move in and out of the White House?

A. If you were going to move into a completely furnished home for four years, what would you take? That is the kind of decision a new first family must make.

A few weeks before the inauguration, the wife of the incoming president visits the White House. She is shown around by the outgoing first lady and the White House staff.

Several days before the inauguration, the outgoing first family moves out some of its personal belongings.

On Inauguration Day, the new president and his family and the vice president and his family and certain members of Congress arrive at the White House. The outgoing president escorts the president-elect to the Capitol.

While the inauguration ceremony is going on, a moving van arrives and unloads the new first family's belongings.

After the ceremony and parade, members of the first family just walk into the White House. They don't even have to bring sheets and towels.

Q. What can first families move in?

A. First families can bring any furnishings they wish for the family living quarters on the second and third floors.

They are allowed a budget of $50,000 to redecorate these rooms if they wish. Sometimes friends raise money to help pay to redo these rooms.

The Reagans brought furniture from their California home to make their second floor study more comfortable.

80

Furniture

President Arthur added this glass screen to the Entrance Hall. It is no longer there.

Q. Where do they get the White House furniture?

A. "I will not live in a house like this," said Chester A. Arthur. He had inspected the shabby furniture and decorations.

For many years, presidents were allowed to sell the White House furnishings and use the money to buy other things for it.

President Arthur sold some 24 wagonloads of battered furniture. Today there is a law that the official White House furniture cannot be sold.

Furnishings not on display, those that are valuable because of their history or because they are fine art, are kept in a storage facility. Presidents and their families may select furniture for the private rooms from this collection. However, on changes to the public rooms, the president is advised by a special committee.

This chair and a few other pieces of furniture for the Blue Room were purchased by James Monroe after the fire.

Q. How long has most of the furniture visitors see on the tour been at the White House?

A. Most of it has been acquired for the White House in the past 40 years. First lady Jacqueline Kennedy started the White House Historical Association. This organization provides funds to buy art and furniture for the White House.

White House Collection

Like a lot of the White House china, the Reagan china has the presidential seal on it.

The Hayes china had American birds and plants painted on it.

Q. Does each president get a new set of china?

A. Presidents have been given money by Congress to buy new china if they wish. Sometimes friends of the president buy new china with money that they contribute. Any china that a president buys becomes a part of the White House collection.

This was not always the case. For the first 100 years, presidents could sell sets that were broken or cracked. The money from the sale could be used to buy new china. A lot of china was disposed of.

Today cracked china is broken into tiny pieces and discarded. This stops souvenir hunters from getting and reselling it.

81

Staying at the White House

Q. What would it be like to be an overnight guest at the White House?
A. If a member of the first family invited you to spend the night at the White House, you would be a guest in the family living area on the second and third floors.

You would first have to go through security. You would be met by an escort who would lead you through the ground floor to an elevator and up to the second floor. The elevator can hold about six people.

Being upstairs is much like being in a very fine private home.

Gerald Ford, with family and friends, celebrates his birthday in the hall on the second floor.

Your bedroom would be on the second or third floor. You might sleep in the Queen's Bedroom.

You might go swimming, bowling, or see a movie in the White House theater.

These visitors are trying out comfortable seats in the family movie theater.

You might eat in the family dining room on the second floor. Some visitors eat in the third-floor solarium, or family room. Others might eat in sitting rooms off their bedrooms.

BREAKFAST MENU

Tea _____   Orange Juice _____
Coffee: regular _____   Tomato Juice _____
  decaffeinated _____   Grapefruit Juice _____

Grapefruit Sections _____
Melon (If available.) _____

Toast _____ Bran Muffin _____ English Muffin _____
Jellies: Marmalade _____
  Grape _____
  Strawberry _____

Cereal   Hot _____ Cold _____

Eggs: Fried _____   Poached _____
  Scrambled _____   Soft Boiled _____

Bacon _____   Sausage _____

Pancakes _____

SPECIAL INSTRUCTIONS

Please serve at _____ A.M.
  Bedroom _____
  Dining Room _____
  Solarium _____

NAME _____

You might eat in the private dining room, or in your room. Here is a White House room service order blank. What would you choose?

82

Dining in

The Nixon family in the second floor dining room.

Q. Does the White House have "room service"?

A. The White House does have room service. The president and his houseguests can order a sandwich or something to drink. However, once the president goes to bed, room service is no longer available.

Q. Can members of the first family order in pizza?

A. Yes, but they would not pick up the phone and order it. A member of the staff would go and pick it up. Of course, the pizza restaurant would not know who it was for.

Shopping

Q. Does the first family go shopping for clothes and presents?

A. Not usually. Most of the time someone does it for them, or designers or store managers bring in clothes for them to try on.

Big dinners

Q. Who pays for the big dinners?

A. The president does not pay for most big dinners. They are paid for by the part of the government that the president is entertaining. For example, the State Department pays for the state dinners. There are about nine of these each year.

An example of a beautiful table setting for an elegant state dinner.

Fancy food

Q. Since presidents can order what they wish, do they often eat fancy food?

A. While first families can order what they wish, many members watch their diet.

Some presidents like very simple meals. For lunch, Richard Nixon liked cottage cheese with ketchup. Gerald Ford liked cottage cheese for lunch and butter pecan ice cream for dessert.

The chief usher inspects the dinner tables set up in the Blue Room.

An assistant usher shows these visitors her computer. She works in the usher's office near the front door of the White House.

Q. Who hires the people who work in the White House?

A. The person in charge of the White House residence staff is called the chief usher. This job title can be traced back to the time when James Buchanan was president.

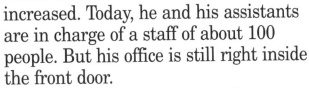

Ushers knew who came and went.

Over the years, the chief usher's duties have increased. Today, he and his assistants are in charge of a staff of about 100 people. But his office is still right inside the front door.

The chief usher and his staff know exactly how to handle each event. They have lists of what to do and when. These planning lists are called "scenarios." The White House has scenarios for just about every occasion.

While presidents come and go, many White House employees work there for years. They know where things are and how things should be done.

White House employees feel a great sense of pride in serving their country, the president and his family.

The staff can be of great help to new families moving in.

Working at the White House demands teamwork. Over the years, each team member has known how to do things in the "White House way." There is a high standard of excellence.

"You're working for the highest office in the land. You know that whatever you do is going to affect the family upstairs," said former doorman Preston Bruce.

84

Q. How do they keep the White House clean?

A. Keeping the White House sparkling clean is a big job. Cleaning crews work late into the night after a big dinner. The house must be ready for tours early in the morning.

A window washer is always on the job in some part of the house. Chandeliers are cleaned about four times a year. It takes a day to clean each of three big ones in the East Room. Each crystal is polished one at a time.

Scout's WHITE HOUSE WORKERS
Word Search

Words that remind us of workers at the White House are hidden in the block below. Some words are hidden backward. See if you can find: BUTLER, MAID, ENGINEER, DOORMAN, CARPENTER, PLUMBER, SEAMSTRESS, CHEF, COOK, MESSENGER, FLORIST, USHER, FURNITURE, CLEANER, CURATOR, PRIDE, LOYAL, HONOR, POLISH.

WOULD YOU LIKE TO WORK IN THE WHITE HOUSE?

```
F R E N A E L C A C O O K G M
U B H R O T A R U C C H E F E
R R E T N E P R A C C I P D S
N U S H E R R E L T U B L O S
I L O Y A L H S I L O P U O E
T D E D I R P R O N O H M R N
U E J R E E N I G N E K B M G
R M A I D T S I R O L F E A E
E F S S E R T S M A E S R N R
```

© Bill Petros

A houseman makes the White House cleaning schedules.

Grocery shopping

Q. Who does the grocery shopping?

A. Specially trained storekeepers do the shopping. They shop at several approved stores and markets. Secret Service agents check out the groceries before they are delivered.

President William Henry Harrison would sometimes take his basket and walk to market himself.

F. W. Brouard

The Easter Egg Roll

Q. When did the Easter Egg Roll start?

A. The Easter Egg Roll was started in 1878 by President Hayes and his wife. Children used to bring their own eggs and roll them on the White House lawn. Today the eggs are furnished.

The Easter Egg Roll attracts thousands of children each year.

Cooking

The pastry chef and his assistant show these visitors a sample of the White House pastries.

Q. Who does the cooking?

A. The White House has several chefs. They are among the best in the world. The president pays the bill for the food served to the family and its guests. He does not have to pay the chefs.

Social secretaries

A social secretary gives last-minute instructions to military aides.

Q. Who are social secretaries and what do they do?

A. Social secretaries are women who help the first lady manage and plan her busy social schedule.

Social secretaries have a staff. They also have the assistance of military social aides. These are members of the armed forces who greet visitors and make them feel at home.

Military social aides are unmarried officers who usually work at the White House for about two years. For them, it is not a full-time job. They do their regular military duties in addition to their White House service.

A Park Service employee works outside to get the South Portico steps ready for an event.

White House Photo

© Bill Petros

The White House curator shows a visitor a famous piece of sculpture by western artist Frederic Remington. The curator's job is to keep track of and care for the furnishings and art.

Q. Who are some of the other people who work at the White House?

A. Over the years, different government departments have taken over certain duties at the White House. For example, the president has a valet who is in the military. The military also handles transportation and communication. The National Park Service looks after the grounds.

For many years presidents had to pay for the White House servants and entertaining out of their own pockets. Finally in 1897, Congress passed a law that gave the president a certain amount to pay these expenses.

Abby's White House "How Manys"

To do: Ask a family member or a friend if he or she can guess how many of these things the main part of the White House has.

1. Bedrooms . . . . _____

2. Fireplaces . . . . _____

3. Doors. . . . . _____

4. Bathrooms . . . . _____

5. Closets. . . . . _____

6. Kitchens . . . . _____

7. Elevators. . . . . _____

8. Windows . . . . _____

Answers: 1. 11, 2. 28, 3. 412, 4. 32, 5. 17, 6. 4, 7. 5, 8. 147.

Q. We often hear, "The White House says ..." What does that mean?

A. We all know that the White House can't talk. When we hear that "the White House says" this or that, a member of the president's staff is being quoted.

There are really two different staffs at the White House. One works for whoever is president. These staff members usually leave their White House jobs when the president goes out of office.

The other White House staff is in charge of the building and of serving the first family. Many have been at the White House for a long time.

Q. What is the president's salary while he is in office?

A. The president makes $400,000 a year. He also pays no rent, water or electricity bills while he and his family live in the White House.

Abby's White House Recipe

White House Sugar Cookies

Here's a recipe from White House pastry chef Roland Mesnier.

You'll need:
- 1 cup butter
- $1\frac{1}{2}$ cups sugar
- 2 eggs
- 1 teaspoon vanilla
- $3\frac{1}{2}$ cups all-purpose flour
- $\frac{1}{2}$ teaspoon salt
- $\frac{1}{2}$ teaspoon baking powder

What to do:

1. In a large bowl, mix butter and sugar until smooth and creamy.

2. Add eggs and vanilla. Mix well.

3. Add remaining ingredients. Mix well.

4. Flatten dough onto a sheet pan lined with plastic wrap.

5. Refrigerate at least 2 hours.

6. Roll dough onto a floured pastry cloth and cut into shapes.

7. Bake in a preheated 350-degree oven for eight to 10 minutes or until slightly golden brown.

Scout's Maze

In the maze at right, help Scout find his ticket for the White House tour.

The Presidents and Their First Ladies

1. George Washington 1789-1797

Martha Washington

2. John Adams 1797-1801

Abigail Adams

National Gallery of Art

3. Thomas Jefferson 1801-1809

Martha Randolph (daughter)

Department of State, Diplomatic Reception Room

All of the Presidents' and first ladies' portraits in this section are from the White House Collection unless otherwise indicated.

4. James Madison 1809-1817

Dolley Madison

5. James Monroe 1817-1825

Elizabeth Monroe

Thomas J. Edwards and William K. Edwards

6. John Quincy Adams 1825-1829

Louisa Catherine Adams

7. Andrew Jackson 1829-1837

Emily Donelson (niece)

8. Martin Van Buren 1837-1841

Angelica Van Buren (daughter-in-law)

9. William Henry Harrison 1841

Anna Harrison

**10. John Tyler
1841-1845**

© John Tyler Griffin

**Letitia Tyler
(died in 1842)**

Julia Tyler

**11. James K.
Polk
1845-1849**

Sarah Polk

James K. Polk
Ancestral Home

**12. Zachary
Taylor
1849-1850**

**Betty Taylor
Bliss
(daughter)**

Smithsonian Institution

**13. Millard
Fillmore
1850-1853**

**Abigail
Fillmore**

**14. Franklin
Pierce
1853-1857**

Jane Pierce

Pierce Brigade

**15. James
Buchanan
1857-1861**

**Harriet Lane
(niece)**

Smithsonian Institution

**16. Abraham
Lincoln
1861-1865**

**Mary Todd
Lincoln**

Lloyd Ostendorf
Collection

**17. Andrew
Johnson
1865-1869**

Smithsonian Institution

Eliza Johnson

Andrew Johnson National
Historic Site

**Martha Johnson
Patterson (daughter)**

**18. Ulysses
S. Grant
1869-1877**

Julia Grant

Library of Congress

90

19. Rutherford B. Hayes 1877-1881

Lucy Hayes

20. James Garfield 1881

Lucretia Garfield

Library of Congress

21. Chester A. Arthur 1881-1885

Mary Arthur McElroy (sister)

22. Grover Cleveland 1885-1889

Smithsonian Institution

Rose Cleveland (sister)

Frances Cleveland

23. Benjamin Harrison 1889-1893

Caroline Harrison

24. Grover Cleveland 1893-1897

Frances Cleveland

Smithsonian Institution

25. William McKinley 1897-1901

Ida McKinley

26. Theodore Roosevelt 1901-1909

Edith Roosevelt

27. William Howard Taft 1909-1913

Helen Taft

28. Woodrow Wilson 1913-1921

Sarah Hightower Regional Library

Ellen Wilson (died in 1914)

Edith Wilson

29. Warren Harding 1921-1923

Florence Harding

30. Calvin Coolidge 1923-1929

Grace Coolidge

31. Herbert Hoover 1929-1933

Lou Hoover

32. Franklin D. Roosevelt 1933-1945

Eleanor Roosevelt

33. Harry S. Truman 1945-1953

Bess Truman

34. Dwight D. Eisenhower 1953-1961

Mamie Eisenhower

35. John F. Kennedy 1961-1963

Jacqueline Kennedy

36. Lyndon Johnson 1963-1969

Lady Bird Johnson

37. Richard M. Nixon 1969-1974

Pat Nixon

38. Gerald Ford 1974-1977

Betty Ford

39. James E. Carter 1977-1981

Rosalynn Carter

40. Ronald W. Reagan 1981-1989

Nancy Reagan

41. George Bush 1989-1993

Barbara Bush

42. Bill Clinton 1993-2001

Hillary Rodham Clinton

43. George W. Bush 2001-

Laura Welch Bush

Go dot to dot and color.

How to Visit the White House

ALL TICKETS ARE FREE.

THE WHITE HOUSE IS OPENED FOR TOURS TUESDAY THROUGH SATURDAY.

There are two ways to get tickets to visit the White House. Every effort is made to keep the waiting time as short as possible.

1. For Guided Tours:

The U.S. Capitol Building

Parents and other adults can contact their member of Congress at his or her local or Washington office. These tours are Tuesday through Saturday, starting between 8:00 and 9:00 a.m.

They last about 30 minutes and are guided by tour officers of the U.S. Secret Service.

Your member of Congress will mail you your tickets. Write to request tickets at least two months before the tour date.

2. For Self-Guided Tours:

THE WHITE HOUSE
WASHINGTON

If someone wants to pick up tickets for a family, the limit is four tickets per person, per day. The tickets are valid only on the day they are issued.

Each ticket has the time when the tour begins at the bleachers on the Ellipse, a park south of the White House.

Tourists can pick up tickets at the White House Visitor Center at 1450 Pennsylvania Ave., N.W., Washington, D.C. Park Service rangers will answer questions and issue tickets.

During peak season, tickets are timed for entry between 10 a.m. and noon. They are available only on the day of the tour on a first-come, first-served basis starting at 7:30 a.m. It's best to get there early. Each person, including children, needs a ticket.

After visitors get their ticket time, they can leave the area but should return in time to get to the bleachers to begin the tour.

No parking is available for White House tourists. Visitors might want to take the Metro, or subway.

94

To get the most out of a visit to the White House, go to the Visitor Center first. It is run by the National Park Service.

All visitors must go through a security check operated by members of the Secret Service. The Secret Service is in charge of guarding the president and his family.

The Visitor Center is open from 7:30 a.m. to 4 p.m. It also has a museum shop operated by the White House Historical Association.

During some parts of the year, tickets are not necessary. You just get in line at the south visitors' entrance.

Your tour

Visitors begin the tour by entering the East Visitors' Entrance. National Park Service rangers check tickets, keep the line moving and answer questions.

Visitors walk up the curved driveway into the East Wing. Members of the uniformed Secret Service are on guard.

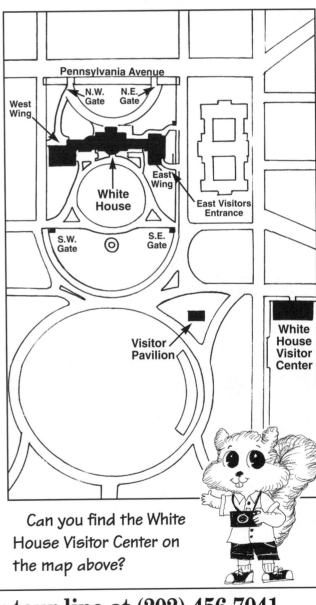

Can you find the White House Visitor Center on the map above?

All visitors can call the 24-hour tour line at (202) 456-7041 for the latest information.

This view shows the South Portico, or porch. It overlooks the big back yard of the White House.

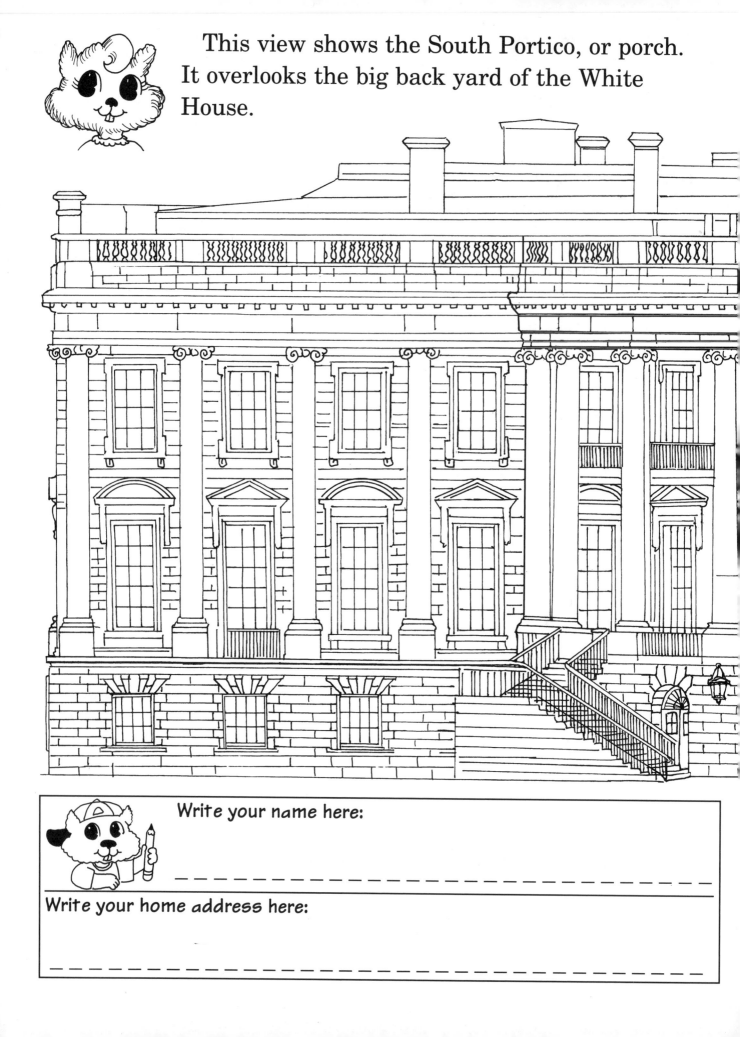

Write your name here:

_ _

Write your home address here:

_ _